D1577919

Presented to

_____

by

_____

on

_____

Read Together Bible

Read Together Bible

Stories retold by
Bonnie Bruno and Carol Reinsma
Illustrated by Jenifer Schneider

Standard
PUBLISHING
Bringing The Word to Life™

Cincinnati, Ohio

© 2006 Standard Publishing, Cincinnati, Ohio.
A division of Standex International Corporation.
All rights reserved. Printed in China.
Project editor: Laura Derico.
Cover design: Robert Glover. Cover illustration: Martin Lemelman.
Interior design: Sandy Wimmer, Steve Clark.
Text and art appeared previously as *The Young Reader's Bible,*
© 1994, 1998 Standard Publishing.

ISBN 0-7847-1741-9

12 11 10 09 08 07 06   9 8 7 6 5 4 3 2 1

You read to me,
    I'll read to you.
        We can read together too!
    One reads orange words
And one reads blue.
        And the green words can be read by two!

Contents

The Old Testament

The Beginning 12

Man and Woman. 16

Evil Enters Eden 20

Water, Water Everywhere 24

A Surprise for Sarah 28

A Very Hairy Trick 32

A Pillow and a Promise 36

Sold! A Sneaky Deal 40

Double Dreams 44

God Meant It for Good 48

Baby Moses' Riverboat. 52

I Am Sending You. 56

Ten Terrible Troubles 60

Pharaoh's Biggest Mistake. 64

A Special Treasure. 68

Faith or Fear?. 72

Seven Times and a Shout. 76

Torches and Trumpets 80

Strong Samson. 84

Ruth's Rich Reward 88

A Voice in the Dark. 92

A New King for Israel 96

A Giant Problem 100

The King Who Sang Praises 104

Solomon's One Wish 108

Meals for the Messenger 112

The Lord, He Is God! 116

In a Chariot of Fire 120

A Gulp and a Great City 124

Three Brave Friends 128

Daniel for Dinner? 132

A Plan and a Party 136

Remember and Obey 140

The Promised One 144

The New Testament

The Man with No Voice 150

Mary Meets an Angel 154

His Name Is John 158

One Night in Bethlehem 162

Good News of Great Joy 166

Follow That Star! 170

Taller and Wiser 174

The Right Thing to Do 178

Jesus' Team of 12 182

Inside and Out 186

Jesus the Teacher 190

Just Say the Word 194

Wild Winds and Waves Obey . . .198

Enough for Everyone 202

Peter Takes a Walk 206

Now I See 210

A Neighbor Shows Kindness . . .214

Teach Us to Pray 218

Lost and Found 222

Lazarus Lives Again 226

One Thankful Man 230

Let the Children Come 234

Big News for a Little Man 238

Praise to the King of Kings! 242

Remember Me 246

A Sad, Dark Night 250

King of a Different Kingdom . . .254

Could It Be True? 258

It Is True! 262

Parting Promises 266

The Very First Church 270

Jumping for Joy 274

Saul Sees the Light 278

Timothy Joins the Journey 282

The Night the Prison Shook 286

Come Quickly, Lord Jesus! 290

The Old Testament

The Beginning

from Genesis 1 and 2

God is the beginning of all things.

God made the heavens and the earth.

**The earth was empty and dark,
with water everywhere.**

**Then God said, "Let there be light."
And there was!**

**There was evening and morning.
This was the first day.**

**Next, God put a wide space
above the water.**

**God called the space sky.
This was the second day.**

On the third day,
God gathered
the water into
its own places.

Now there were
seas and dry ground.

"Let plants grow in the ground,"
God said. And they did!

Then God said,
"Let there be
lights in the sky
for day and
for night."

God made the sun,
the moon, and the stars.
This was the fourth day.

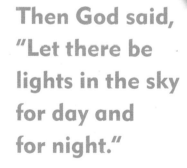

**On the fifth day, God made fish
for the seas. He made birds for the sky.**

**On the sixth day,
God made living things for the land.**

Then God said,"Let us make
human beings. Let them rule over
the fish of the sea, the birds of the air,
and the living things on land."

God made the first human being from the dust.

**The first man was called Adam.
God breathed into Adam the breath of life.**

**God looked at all he had made.
It was very good!**

On the seventh day, God rested.
He made that day a holy day.

Man and Woman

from Genesis 2

God planted a garden in a place called Eden.

Trees grew in the garden.

The trees were beautiful,
and some had fruit that was good for food.

A river watered the garden. God put Adam
in the garden to take care of it.

"You may eat the fruit
from any tree in the garden
except one," said God.
"If you eat from the tree
of knowing good and evil,
you will die."

God also said,
"It is not good for Adam to be alone."

So God brought
all the birds and animals to Adam.

Adam gave each one a name.

But none of these creatures
was the right helper for Adam.

So God made Adam fall into a deep sleep.

Then God made a woman
from Adam's rib.
God brought her to Adam.

Adam said, "Here is someone like me.
Her bones came from my bones.
Her body came from my body.
I will call her woman,
because she was taken out of man."

19

Evil Enters Eden

from Genesis 3

One day a sneaky snake came to the woman.

"Did God really tell you not to eat fruit from any tree in the garden?" asked the snake.

"God told us we may eat fruit
from all the trees except one," said Eve.
"God told us we will die
if we eat from that tree."

"You will not die," said the snake.
"You will be like God.
You will know good and evil."

The fruit on the tree looked good to eat.

Eve took some and ate it.

Then she gave some
to Adam,
and he ate it, too.

Then Adam and Eve saw
that they were naked.

They made coverings for themselves.

Soon they heard God walking through the garden.
Quickly, they hid.

"Where are you?" God called.
"Did you eat from the tree?"

"The woman you put here
gave me the fruit," said Adam.

"The snake tricked me,
and I ate it," said Eve.

"From now on you will crawl
on your belly," God told the snake.

Then God made clothes for Adam and Eve.

Sadly, he sent them out of the garden.

"Your work will cause you pain," God said.
"And when you die,
your body will turn back to dust."

Water, Water Everywhere

from Genesis 6 – 9

Soon many people lived
on earth.

But everywhere God looked,
people were sinning.

Only Noah loved God.

"I am going to send a big flood,"
God told Noah.
"Water will cover the whole earth.
Every living thing will die."

Noah listened carefully.

"I want you to build
an ark," said God.

Noah obeyed God.
Two of every kind of animal
came to Noah to live on the ark.

Then Noah and his family went inside.
God closed the door, and the rain began.

God sent rain for 40 days.
Water covered the whole world.

**Then Noah sent out a dove
to look for dry land.**

And one day, the dove did not come back.

"It is time to go out now!" called Noah.

Noah and his family thanked God
for keeping them safe.

God was pleased.
He put a beautiful rainbow in the sky.

"This is a sign of my promise,"
said God. "I will never send
another flood like this one."

A Surprise for Sarah

from Genesis 12, 15, 18, and 21

God told Abraham
to leave his country.

"I will bless you
in a new **land**," God said.

Abraham obeyed. He took his wife,
his servants, and his flocks.

"Can you count the stars?"
God asked Abraham.

There were too many to count!

"So shall your family be," said God.

"But I have no children," said Abraham.

"Don't worry," said God.
"I will give you a son."

One day, God sent
three visitors.

"Please rest under my tree," said Abraham.

"Where is Sarah, your wife?"
asked one visitor.

"In the tent," said Abraham.

"Sarah is going to have a son,"
said the visitor.

Sarah heard the news.
She laughed to herself.

"Abraham and I are too old
to have a baby," she said.

The visitor knew that Sarah laughed.

"Is anything too hard for God?"
he said.

God kept his promise.
The next year,
baby Isaac was born!
Abraham was 100
when he held his newborn son.

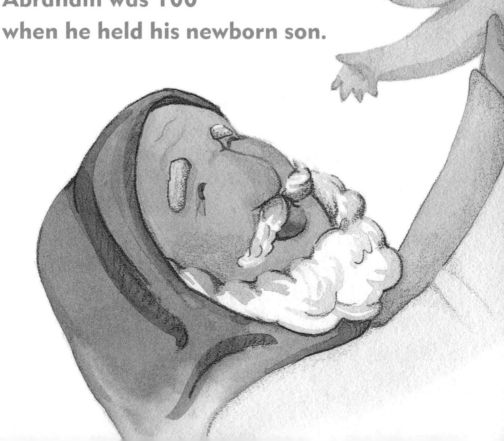

Sarah laughed out loud this time.

"Everyone who hears about this
will be happy for us!" she said.

A Very Hairy Trick

from Genesis 25, 27, and 28

God gave twin boys
to Isaac and his wife, Rebekah.

Esau grew up to be
a hunter. He was a hairy man.

Jacob liked to do quiet work
at home around the tents.

By then, Isaac was very old.

It was time for him
to give his blessing to
Esau, his firstborn son.

But Rebekah planned a trick.

Rebekah cooked
Isaac's favorite meal.

"Put on Esau's clothes,"
she told Jacob.
"Put these animal skins
on your hands and neck.
Now take this food
to your father."

Isaac was blind,
but he held Jacob's hands
and felt the hairy skins.
He smelled Esau's clothes.

The trick worked.
After Isaac ate,
he gave
his blessing
to Jacob.

33

Esau also brought food to Isaac.

"Give me your blessing now," he said.

Then Isaac knew he had been tricked.

Esau was sad and angry. "My own brother has stolen my blessing!" he cried.

Rebekah was afraid.
"Esau may hurt you," she told Jacob.
"You must leave." So Jacob left home
to live with his uncle in another land.

A Pillow and a Promise

from Genesis 28, 32, and 33

On his way to see his uncle, Jacob stopped to sleep.

He used a stone for a pillow.

While Jacob slept,
God sent him a special dream.

In his dream, Jacob saw angels
going up and down a tall ladder.

The ladder led to heaven. At the top stood God.

God spoke to Jacob in the dream.

"I am the God of Abraham
and the God of Isaac," he said.
"I will give this land
to you and all your children.
The whole world will be blessed
through your family.
I am with you always," said God.
"You do not need to be afraid."

Jacob woke up.
"Surely God is in this place!" he said.

In the morning, Jacob took his stone pillow
and set it up as a pillar.
He poured oil over it.

Many years passed. Jacob began
a trip home to see his father, Isaac.

**But Jacob was still afraid
of his brother.**

Jacob sent Esau a message.
And Jacob asked God for help.

Jacob bowed down when he saw Esau.

**But Esau ran with open arms
to meet his brother.**

The brothers hugged
and cried happy tears.
Jacob gave Esau a present.
It felt good to be going home!

Sold! A Sneaky Deal

from Genesis 35 and 37

**Jacob had 12 sons,
but he loved Joseph the most.**

**Jacob gave Joseph
a wonderful coat.**

Joseph's brothers were jealous.

"Listen to my dreams," said Joseph.
"In the field, my bundle of grain
stood up straight. Your bundles bowed
down to mine.
Then I dreamed
the sun and the moon
and 11 stars
bowed to me."

"Do you think we will bow down
to you?" said Joseph's brothers.

They were angry. One day Joseph
went to see his brothers in the field.

"Here comes that dreamer," said the brothers.
"Let's get rid of him."

Joseph's brothers tore off his wonderful coat.
They threw him into a pit.

"Look," said a brother. "A group of traders.
Let's sell Joseph to them!"

The traders took Joseph.

Then the brothers
dipped Joseph's coat in goat's blood.
They took the coat to their father.

"Is this Joseph's coat?"
they asked him.

"It is!" cried Jacob. "A wild animal must have killed him."

Jacob cried for many days. No one could comfort him. Meanwhile, Joseph became a slave in Egypt.

Double Dreams

from Genesis 39 – 41

In Egypt, Joseph was put into prison for something he did not do.

The king's cupbearer was put into prison, too.

One morning, the cupbearer said, "I had a strange dream last night. What does it mean?"

"God knows," said Joseph. Joseph told the cupbearer the meaning of his dream.

In three days, the dream came true.

The cupbearer was called back to the palace.

"Remember me," said Joseph.
But the cupbearer forgot.

Two years later, Pharaoh the king
had strange dreams.
The cupbearer remembered Joseph.

"I know a man who can tell
the meaning of dreams," said the cupbearer.

"Send for him," said Pharaoh.

45

Pharaoh told Joseph his dreams.

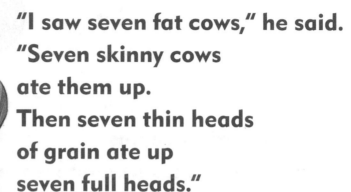

"I saw seven fat cows," he said.
"Seven skinny cows
ate them up.
Then seven thin heads
of grain ate up
seven full heads."

"God gave you two dreams that mean
the same thing," said Joseph.
"There will be seven good years
with plenty of food.
Then there will be seven bad years
with nothing."

"God has made you wise,"
said Pharaoh.
"I will put you
in charge of the land."

For seven years, Joseph saved grain in barns. Then the bad years came.

But there was food in Egypt because Joseph had saved it up.

God Meant It for Good

from Genesis 42 – 47

Joseph's brothers went to Egypt to buy grain.

They saw Joseph there, but they did not know him.

I will find out if my brothers have changed, thought Joseph.

"You are spies," he said.

"No," said the brothers.
"We are honest men.
Our father and our brother Benjamin
are at home."

"Prove that you are honest," said Joseph.
"Go now. Come back with
your brother Benjamin."

The brothers went home.
When their grain was gone,
they came back to Egypt with Benjamin.

This time,
Joseph told
his servant
to hide a silver cup
in Benjamin's bag.

In the morning, Joseph sent his servant after the brother. The silver cup was found in Benjamin's bag.

"Make us your slaves, not Benjamin!" cried the brothers.

Joseph saw that his brothers had changed.

"Come close to me," Joseph said. "I am your brother Joseph."

The brothers shook with fear.

"Don't be upset," said Joseph.
"You wanted to hurt me.
But God meant it for good.
God used me to save you.
Go and bring
our father here."

In a dream,
God promised Jacob
that his family
would become great
in Pharaoh's land.

So Jacob
and all his family
went to live in Egypt.

Baby Moses' Riverboat

from Exodus 1 and 2

Jacob's family, the Hebrews, grew.

"There are too many Hebrews in Egypt," said a new pharaoh.

Pharaoh made the Hebrews slaves, because he was afraid of them.

Pharaoh also made a law.
All new Hebrew baby boys must be killed.

But one Hebrew mother hid her baby in a basket. She floated the basket at the edge of the river.

The princess of Egypt found the little baby.

"This is a Hebrew baby," she said softly.

The baby's sister was watching.
She ran to the princess.

"Shall I find a Hebrew woman
to nurse the baby for you?"

"Yes, please do,"
said the princess.

The girl came back
with the baby's own mother!
Surely God is watching over this baby,
the mother thought.

**The baby's mother took him home
and cared for him.**

When he was older,
his mother took him to the princess.

The princess adopted him as her own son.

"I will call him Moses," she said,
"because I took him out of water."

I Am Sending You

from Exodus 2 – 4

In Egypt, the Hebrews were also called Israelites.

Years earlier,
God had changed Jacob's name to Israel.

The Israelites were slaves in Egypt
a long time. But God had a plan for them.

Moses grew up. He left Egypt
and became a shepherd.

In the desert near a mountain,
Moses saw a bush on fire.

"How strange," said Moses.
"The bush is on fire,
but it is not burning up!"

Then God called
to Moses from
the bush.

Moses covered
his face
because
he was afraid
to look at God.

57

"I have heard the cries of my people," said God.
"And I am sending you
to bring them out of Egypt."

"But God, why me?" said Moses.

"I will be with you," said God.

"But what if no one listens to me?" cried Moses.

"Throw your staff down," said God.

The staff became a snake.

"Now pick it up," said God.

The snake became a staff again.

"Show this to the people," said God.

"But I am not a good speaker," said Moses.

"Your brother Aaron will go with you
and help you," God said.

Then Moses started back to Egypt.
And God sent Aaron
to meet Moses in the desert.

Ten Terrible Troubles

from Exodus 5 – 12

Moses and Aaron
told Pharaoh, "God says,
Let my people go
into the desert
to worship me."

"No!" said Pharaoh.
"Why should I obey
your God?"

"Go back to Pharaoh," God said.
"Tell Aaron to throw down his staff."

Aaron's staff became a snake.

"My magicians can do that, too,"
said Pharaoh.

Aaron's staff
swallowed the staffs
of the magicians.

But Pharaoh still
would not let God's people go.

Then God sent troubles
on the Egyptians.

First the water turned to blood.
Then frogs covered the land.

Dust turned into biting gnats.
Flies swarmed everywhere.

All of Egypt's livestock died.
Egypt's people broke out in boils.

Hail killed people, plants, and animals.

Hungry locusts
ate the crops.
Darkness covered Egypt
for three days.

But stubborn
Pharaoh still
would not let
God's people go.

Then God told Moses,
"Every firstborn in Egypt
will die. Even Pharaoh's
firstborn. Tell my people
to roast lamb for
their last meal in Egypt.
Tell them to smear
the blood of the lamb
on their doorframes."

The Israelites obeyed God.

That night the firstborn
of every Egyptian family died.

But no one died in a house
with blood on the doorframe.

"Take your people and flocks, and go!"
Pharaoh cried to Moses.

Pharaoh's Biggest Mistake

from Exodus 12 – 15

The Israelites were free!
God led them along a desert road.

During the day, God went ahead of them
in a pillar of cloud.

At night, God went ahead of them
in a pillar of fire.

But in Egypt, Pharaoh was sorry
he had let God's people go.

"Who will work for me now?" he said.
"We must bring those people back!"

The Israelites were camped
beside the Red Sea.

They screamed when they saw
Pharaoh and his chariots.

But Moses said, "Don't be afraid!
The Lord will fight for you."

The tall cloud moved between the Israelites
and the soldiers.

Then Moses
raised his staff
and pointed it
toward the sea.

God sent a
mighty wind
to part
the water.

65

All night long, the Israelites crossed the Red Sea on dry land while God held back the water.

Pharaoh's army tried to follow the Israelites.

But God told Moses, "Lift your staff again." Moses obeyed.

The water of the sea flowed back into place.

All of Pharaoh's soldiers drowned.

But God's people were safe
on the other side of the sea.

**Moses and the Israelites
sang a song of praise to God.**

**Moses' sister, Miriam, led the women
in a dance.**

The Israelites were ready
to follow God anywhere.

A Special Treasure

from Exodus 16, 17, 19, 20, and 31

In the wilderness, the Israelites became hungry and thirsty.

But God covered the ground with manna bread every morning and sometimes quail for meat.

"Hit that rock with your staff," God told Moses.

Water poured from the rock!

The people camped by a mountain.
Moses went up the mountain to talk to God.

"Tell my people to obey me," God said.
"Then they will be my special treasure."

Moses gave God's message
to the people.
After three days,
he led them out
of the camp to the mountain.

Thick smoke covered
the mountain because
God was there.

God spoke to the people.

He gave them ten commandments.

1. Have no other gods but me.
2. Do not worship idols.
3. Use my name for good.
4. Keep the seventh day a holy day.
5. Love and honor your parents.
6. Do not murder.
7. Be true to your husband or wife.
8. Never take what is not yours.
9. Always be honest.
10. Do not be jealous
    of what others have.

Then Moses went up on the mountain again.

God gave him the ten commandments
on two stone tablets.

Faith or Fear?

from Numbers 13 and 14

God told Moses to send 12 men
to explore the land of Canaan.

"I will give this land
to my people," said God.

"See what the people
are like,"
Moses told the 12 men.
"See what their towns
are like."

After 40 days, the men came back.

"The land is flowing with milk and honey," they said. "Here is its fruit. But the people are strong, and their cities have walls."

Caleb said,
"We should not
be afraid.
We can take
the land."

But other men said,
"The people are stronger than we are.
We can't fight them and win."

God's people grumbled to Moses.
"It would be better if we went back
to Egypt," they said.

Then Caleb and Joshua
stood before the people.

"The Lord will lead us into the land,"
Joshua said. "He will give it to us."

But the people talked about
killing Joshua and Caleb.

God was angry with his people.

"You will live and die
here in the desert," God said.
So it was 40 years
before the people went
into the land of Canaan,
the land God
had promised them.

75

Seven Times and a Shout

from Joshua 5 and 6

The gates of Jericho
were shut tight.
No one went out or in.

Then the angel of the Lord
came to Joshua.

"What does God want to tell me?"
Joshua asked the angel.

"I have given you this city," was God's answer.
"Here is what you must do. March your army
around the city. Do it once a day for six days.
Carry the tablets with the ten commandments
in their special box. Have seven priests
blow trumpets as you march."

God told Joshua that the battle
would be won on the seventh day.

"March around the city seven times
on that day," said God. "On the seventh time,
shout, and the walls will fall down."

Joshua obeyed God.

With the army and the priests,
he marched around the city of Jericho.

Early the next morning, Joshua and the army
and the priests marched again.

They did this for six days.
On the seventh day,
they marched seven times
around the city.

On the seventh time, Joshua called out,
"Shout! For the Lord has given you the city."

The priests gave a loud blast
on the trumpets.
The people shouted.

With a crash,
the walls of Jericho
fell to the ground!

79

Torches and Trumpets

from Judges 6 and 7

After many years in Canaan,
the Israelites stopped obeying God.

So God allowed the people of Midian
to take over the land.

The Israelites had to live in caves.
Finally, they asked God for help.

God sent an angel to Gideon, who was threshing wheat.

"The Lord is with you," the angel said. "Go and save Israel from Midian."

"Lord," said Gideon, "I will put out a piece of wool tonight. In the morning, let me find dew on the wool but not on the ground. Then I will know that you will save Israel."

The next morning, the wool was wet, but the ground was dry.

"Give me one more sign," said Gideon.

The next morning, the wool was dry, but the ground was wet.

God gave Gideon a small army of 300 men.

Each man had a trumpet
and a clay jar with a torch inside.

At night, the army made a circle
around the camp of Midian.

The army blew their trumpets and
smashed their jars.

They shouted, "A sword for the Lord and for Gideon!"

The noise and the torches scared the people of Midian. They ran as fast as they could go.

Strong Samson

from Judges 13, 15, and 16

Again the Israelites stopped obeying God.

**So God allowed
the Philistines
to rule over Israel
for 40 years.**

Then God sent Samson.
God had said
that Samson should
never cut his hair.

For a long time, Samson never did.

**Samson was strong.
He fought a thousand Philistines, and won.**

He carried away
a whole city gate!

Samson met Delilah
and fell in love
with her.

The Philistines
came to Delilah.
"Find out the secret
of Samson's strength,"
they said.
"We will pay you well."

Day after day, Delilah asked Samson
to tell her his secret.

Finally Samson said, "If my hair were cut,
I would lose my strength."

Some Philistines hid
in Delilah's house.

They cut Samson's
hair as he slept.

Then Samson's strength was gone.
The Philistines caught him.

The Philistine kings held a party
in the temple of one of their gods.

They made fun of Samson. Samson prayed,
"Lord, give me strength one more time."

He pushed against the pillars
that held up the temple.

The temple crashed down.

Many Philistines died,
and Samson died with them.

Ruth's Rich Reward

from the Book of Ruth

No rain fell. No wheat grew.
There was no food in Judah.

Elimelech and his wife, Naomi,
and their two sons moved
to the land of Moab, where there was food.

The two sons married two women from Moab.

Their names were Ruth and Orpah.

Later, Elimelech and his sons died.
Naomi, Ruth, and Orpah were left alone.

News came that there was food again
in Judah.

Naomi made plans
to go home.

"Let me go with you,"
said Ruth.
"Your people
will be my people.
And your God
will be my God."

So Ruth left Moab
and went to Bethlehem in Judah
with Naomi.

When they came to Bethlehem,
Naomi and Ruth were poor.

But God's law allowed poor people
to pick up fallen grain.

Ruth gathered grain in a field
that belonged to a man named Boaz.

Ruth was kind to Boaz.

He saw that Ruth was special.

He made plans to marry her.

Ruth became Boaz's wife,
and they had a son, named Obed.
When Obed was old,
he became the grandfather
of the great King David.

A Voice in the Dark

from 1 Samuel 1 – 3

At the tent of worship, Hannah prayed.

**"Give me a son, God," she said.
"I will let him serve you all his life."**

Eli the priest saw Hannah praying.

"Go home and
do not worry," said Eli.

God gave Hannah
a baby boy!
She named him Samuel.

When Samuel was old enough,
Hannah took him to Eli.

"I am the one who asked God
for a son," she said.
"Now I am giving him
back to God."

Then Samuel lived
with Eli, and Hannah
came to visit him.

In the dark one night, Samuel heard a voice.

"Samuel!" called the voice.

Samuel ran to Eli's room.
"Here I am," said Samuel.

"I did not call you," said Eli. "Go back to bed."

The voice called to Samuel three times.

"It is the Lord," said Eli.
"If he calls you again,
say, I am your servant,
and I am listening."

God called Samuel
again.

"I am your servant, and I am listening,"
said Samuel.

God gave Samuel a message for Eli.

As Samuel grew up,
God had more messages for him.

Everyone in Israel knew
that Samuel was God's prophet.

A New King for Israel

from 1 Samuel 15 and 16

King Saul of Israel was not obeying God.

**So God told Samuel, "Go to Bethlehem.
Find the man named Jesse.
I have chosen one of Jesse's sons
to be the next king."**

**Samuel went to Bethlehem.
He found Jesse and his sons.
One son was very handsome.**

**He must be
the one God has chosen,
thought Samuel.**

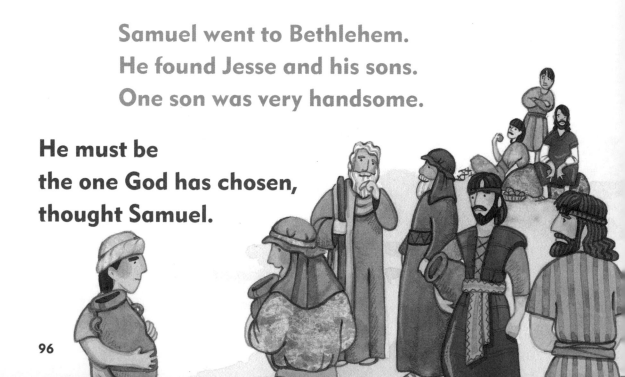

But God told Samuel, "No."

Seven sons stepped forward.

Seven times God said, "This is not the one."

"Do you have any more sons?"
Samuel asked Jesse.

"Yes," said Jesse.
"David is tending the sheep."

Jesse sent for David.

When David came,
God told Samuel,
"This is the one I have chosen.
Anoint him with oil."

After this, an evil spirit
began to bother King Saul.

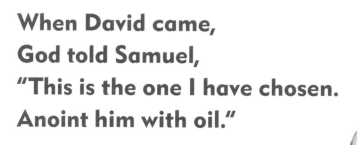

The king's helpers said,
"Music can help you feel better.
A young man named David
plays the harp."

"Send for him,"
said King Saul.

David played his harp for Saul.
The music helped the king.

Saul asked Jesse
to let David live in the palace.

He did not know that someday
David would be king!

99

A Giant Problem

from 1 Samuel 17

Goliath the Philistine was nine feet tall!

Every day for 40 days, Goliath waved his spear and shouted, "Which of you will fight me?"

The Israelites were afraid. No one would fight Goliath.

David's brothers
were soldiers
in Israel's army.

When David came
to visit them,
he saw Goliath
and heard his shouts.

"I am not afraid of Goliath,"
said David.
"I will go and fight him."

"You are just a boy," said King Saul.

"God helped me protect
my sheep from a lion
and a bear," said David.
"God will save me
from Goliath."

King Saul gave David
his own armor.
"At least wear this,"
said Saul.

David took the armor off.
"I am not used to it,"
he said.

David put five smooth stones
in his shepherd's bag.

He carried his staff
and his sling.

"God will give you
over to me today!"
he shouted to Goliath.

David aimed his sling carefully.
With one stone,
he struck Goliath in the forehead.

Goliath fell to the ground with a crash!
The Philistines ran the other way.
And King Saul's army cheered.

The King Who Sang Praises

from 2 Samuel 2 and 5 and Psalms

David became king when Saul died.

David loved to worship God with songs. He wrote many songs himself.

One of David's songs tells how God is like a loving shepherd. *Psalm 23*

Another song tells about God's wonderful creation.

Psalm 24

**Sometimes David told God
about his feelings.** *Psalm 25*

**One of David's songs is about
God's wonderful forgiveness.** *Psalm 32*

**Another song praises God
for knowing David so well.** *Psalm 139*

*The Lord gives me
everything I need.*

*I will not be afraid
because he always protects me.*

*Goodness and love
will always follow me.*

Psalm 23

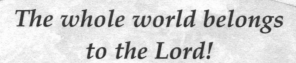

The whole world belongs
to the Lord!

Everything and everyone
are his.

They who seek God are blessed,
for he is the mighty one.

Psalm 24

Look at me and be kind to me.
I am lonely and upset.

I am worried about my problems.
Protect and save me.

I am trusting you.

Psalm 25

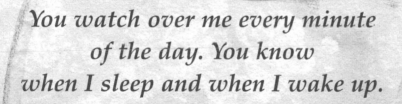

*I confessed my sin
and you forgave me.*

*You have given happiness and
peace back to me!*

*You are full of love, kindness,
and forgiveness.*

Psalm 32

*You watch over me every minute
of the day. You know
when I sleep and when I wake up.*

*You know what I am thinking.
Anywhere I go, you are there.*

*You even knew me before
I was born!*

Psalm 139

Solomon's One Wish

from 1 Kings 2 – 8

When David died, his son Solomon became king.

God spoke to Solomon in a dream.

"Ask me for whatever you want," God said.

Solomon asked for only one thing.

"I need wisdom to be a good king," he said.

God was pleased with Solomon's prayer.

He made Solomon the wisest man
who ever lived.

People from all nations
came to listen to King Solomon.

God gave Israel a time of peace.

"Now we can build a temple where we can worship the Lord," said Solomon.

Thousands of men
cut fine stone and cedar wood for the temple.

Artists carved pictures on the walls.

The inside of the temple was covered with gold.

In seven years, the temple was finished.

The people of Israel
came to the temple to celebrate.

Solomon prayed with them.

Then Solomon said,
"Let us promise
to always obey
the Lord our God."

Meals for the Messenger

from 1 Kings 16 and 17

King Ahab did more evil than any king of Israel before him.

Ahab married Jezebel, who worshiped an idol called Baal.

Ahab set up a place for the people to worship Baal instead of God.

God sent his prophet Elijah
to King Ahab.

"This is a message
from the Lord,"
Elijah told the king.
"There will be no rain or dew
in Israel until I say so."

Ahab wanted to kill Elijah
because of this news from God.

But God told Elijah, "Leave here, go east,
and hide. You will drink from the stream.
And I have told the ravens
to bring you bread
and meat."

Elijah obeyed God.

He hurried to a hiding place and stayed there.

He drank water from the stream.

Every morning and every night,
ravens brought bread and meat to Elijah,
just as God had said.

The Lord, He Is God!

from 1 Kings 18

For three years, there was no rain.

Crops did not grow.

Then God told Elijah,
"Go to King Ahab again.
Soon I will send rain on the land."

When Ahab saw Elijah, he said,
"You are a troublemaker."

"Trouble came because
you did not obey God,"
Elijah said. "Now call the people
to meet me on the mountain.
It is time to choose
between the Lord and Baal."

Elijah asked for two bulls.

"Call on the name of your god,"
Elijah told the people. "I will call on the Lord.
The god who answers by fire, he is God."

The 450 priests of Baal
put one bull
on Baal's altar.

The priests called
on their god
all day.
Nothing
happened.

They called louder.

They cut themselves with swords.

Still there was no answer.

Then Elijah fixed God's altar.

He put the bull on the altar and poured water all around.

"O Lord," prayed Elijah, "let everyone know that *you* are God."

The fire of the Lord burned up the bull, the wood, the stones, and the soil.

It licked up all the water.

The people fell down and cried,
"The Lord, he is God!"
Then the rain came.

In a Chariot of Fire

from 1 Kings 19 and 2 Kings 2

God told Elijah, "Go and make Elisha your helper. Someday, Elisha will take your place as my prophet."

Elijah found Elisha. He was plowing with oxen.

As a sign, Elijah put his coat around Elisha.

Elisha left his plowing and became Elijah's helper.

The day came for Elisha to take Elijah's place.

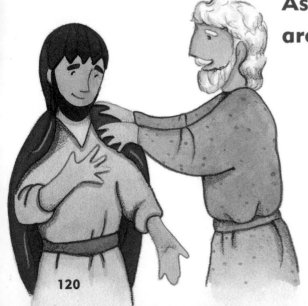

At the Jordan River, Elijah rolled up his coat.

He hit the water with his coat, and
the water parted.

Elijah and Elisha walked
across a dry path.

"If you see me
as I leave,"
said Elijah,
"you will know
that God will
bless you."

A chariot of fire took Elijah into heaven.
Elisha saw it!

Elisha tore his clothes in sadness.
Then he rolled up Elijah's coat.

He struck the water in the river
and the water parted.

"The blessing of God is on Elisha,"
the group of prophets said. They went
to meet him and bowed to him.

A Gulp and a Great City

from the Book of Jonah

"Go to the great city of Nineveh,"
God said to Jonah. "Tell the people to change
their wicked ways."

Jonah did not want
to preach to the
people of Nineveh.

He ran to the sea
and got on a boat.

God sent a storm
on the sea.
The sailors
thought the boat
would break.

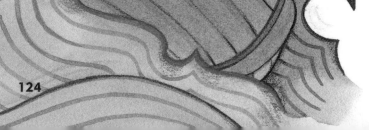

"I am running away from God,
who made the heavens, the sea, and the land,"
Jonah told the sailors. "Throw me
into the sea and the storm will stop."

God sent a great fish
to swallow Jonah.

Inside the fish, Jonah prayed.

After three days,
God told the fish to spit
Jonah out onto the land.

"Go to Nineveh,"
God told Jonah.

This time Jonah obeyed.

"Stop doing evil or God will destroy
your city," Jonah told the people.

The people and the king listened to Jonah
and obeyed God.

And God
saved
their city.

Three Brave Friends

from Daniel 1 and 3

The army of Babylon fought a long battle with God's people, the Jews. Babylon won.

Shadrach, Meshach, and Abednego, three friends who loved God, were taken prisoner to Babylon.

The king of Babylon did not believe in the one true God.

He tried to build a god of his own— a huge golden statue.

"Everyone must bow down
and worship the statue," said the king.
"If you do not, you will be thrown
into a fiery furnace!"

Everyone obeyed the king—but not
Shadrach, Meshach, and Abednego.

"You may have one more chance,"
said the king.

"Never!" said the three brave
friends. "Our God is able
to help us."

Soldiers tied up the three friends
and threw them
into the furnace.

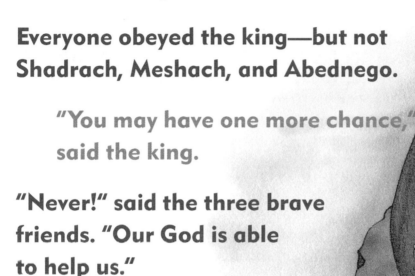

Suddenly the king shouted,
"Look! There are *four* in the fire.
And one of them looks like
a son of the gods!"

The three friends
were let out of the fiery furnace.

They were not burned.

"Blessed be the God of Shadrach,
Meshach, and Abednego!"
cried the king.
"No other god can save in this way!"

Daniel for Dinner?

from Daniel 6

Daniel was the king's favorite helper.

The king's other helpers were jealous of Daniel.

They tricked King Darius into making a new law:

"Pray only to the king for 30 days, or be thrown into the lions' den."

Daniel heard about the new law. But Daniel loved God.

He kept praying to God,
three times every day.

The king's helpers
spied on Daniel.
Then they ran to tell the king.

"Daniel broke the law!"
said the king's helpers.

King Darius was sad.
"Do what must be done," he said.

Daniel was tossed
into a den of hungry lions.

He could not escape.
And the king
could not sleep.

In the morning,
the king hurried to the lions' den.

"Daniel!" he called.
"Has your God rescued you?"

"Yes!" said Daniel.
"The lions did not eat me.
God sent an angel
to shut their mouths!"

The king set Daniel free.
Then he made a brand-new law:

"Everyone must worship Daniel's God,
for he is strong and lives forever!"

A Plan and a Party

from the Book of Esther

The king of Persia chose Esther
for his queen.

The king did not know
that Esther was a Jew.

Esther's cousin, Mordecai,
became one of the king's helpers.

But Mordecai would not bow to Haman,
the chief helper.

Haman learned
that Mordecai was a Jew.
Haman made a plan.

"A group in your kingdom
does not obey your laws,"
Haman told the king.
"We should destroy them."

"Make a law to do it," the king told Haman.

Mordecai heard the news.
He tore his clothes in sadness.

Then he sent a message to Esther.
"Go to the king.
Beg him to help our people."

Esther put on her royal robes.

She stood before the king.

"What can I do for you?" he asked.

"Come to my feast," Esther said.
"Bring Haman, too.
Then I will tell you what I want."

At the feast, Esther told the king
about the plan to kill her people.

"Who has done this?"
the king asked.

"It is Haman,"
Esther said.

The king told
Esther and Mordecai
to write a new law.

The Jews were allowed to fight
and protect themselves.

Haman was put to death.

And all the
Jews in Persia
had a party.

Remember and Obey

from the Book of Nehemiah

Nehemiah was a Jew who worked for the king of Persia.

Nehemiah's brother came to visit.

"The city of Jerusalem has broken walls and burned gates," he said. "The people are sad and afraid."

"Please, God," prayed Nehemiah. "Please help your people."

"Why are you so sad?"
the king asked Nehemiah.

"My city has broken walls
and burned gates,"
said Nehemiah.
"The people are sad and afraid."

"You may go and help them," said the king.

Nehemiah went to Jerusalem.
"Come, let us fix this wall!" he called.
"God will help us."

Enemies tried to stop the work.
But each day, half the men worked
and half kept enemies away.

The wall was finished in 52 days.

Then the laws **God** gave to Moses
were read out loud.

The people were sad
because they had not obeyed God's laws.

But Nehemiah said, "This is a happy day,
because now you *want* to obey God."

The people sang and feasted.

They promised to remember God
and always to obey him.

143

The Promised One

from Psalms, Isaiah, Micah, and Zechariah

God promised his people that he would send a Savior to help them.

God told his promises to his prophets, who wrote the promises down.

For hundreds of years before the Savior came, God's people read the promises and hoped he would come soon.

A child will be born.

A son will be given.

He will be called Wonderful Counselor, Mighty God, Everlasting Father, and Prince of Peace.

Isaiah 9

O Bethlehem, even though
you are small, out of you will come
for me one who will rule Israel.

Micah 5

His peace will never end.
In his kingdom will be
everything that is right.

Isaiah 9

He will be born from a virgin.
You will call him Immanuel,
which means "God with us."

Isaiah 7

He will die like someone
who is evil.

He will be counted with those
who have done wrong things.

His death will take away sins.

Isaiah 53

We will look at him
and be full of sadness.

But God will protect him.
Not one of his bones will be broken.

Zechariah 12, Psalm 34

He will chase away all sadness.
The people who walk
in darkness will see a great light.

Isaiah 9

The New Testament

The Man with No Voice

from Luke 1

Zechariah and his wife, Elizabeth, had never had a child.

And now they were far too old.

But one day, Zechariah was in the temple, burning incense to the Lord.

Then an angel came. Zechariah was afraid!

But the angel said, "Don't be afraid, Zechariah. God has heard your prayer. Soon you and Elizabeth will have a son. You will name him John."

The angel told Zechariah more about John.

"He will bring you joy," the angel said.
"He will lead many people back to God.
And he will prepare the way
for the coming of the Lord."

Zechariah was
puzzled.

"How do I know
all of this
will come true?"
he asked.

"I am Gabriel," the angel said.
"I stand before God. He has sent me
to tell you the news about John.
Now you will not be able to talk
until all of this happens,
because you did not believe me."

Outside the temple,
people waited for Zechariah.

When he came out, he had no voice.

He made signs to the people.

"Surely he has seen a vision!"
the people said.

Mary Meets an Angel

from Luke 1

Young Mary of Nazareth
was engaged to marry Joseph.

But before the wedding day,
the angel Gabriel came.

"Hello, Mary," said the angel.
"The Lord is with you."

What does this mean?
wondered Mary.

"Don't be afraid,"
the angel said.
"You have found
favor with God."

Gabriel had big news for Mary.

"You are going to have a baby boy,"
he said. "You will name him Jesus.
He will be great,
and his kingdom will never end."

"How can this be?" asked Mary.
"I don't have a husband."

"God's Holy Spirit will come upon you,"
said the angel. "That is why the baby will
be called the Son of God."

The angel said, "And your cousin Elizabeth is having a child, even though she is old. Nothing is impossible with God."

"I have always loved God," Mary said quietly. "And I will be his servant. Let everything happen just as you have said."

Then the angel left as quickly as he had appeared.

His Name Is John

from Luke 1

Mary was eager
to tell Elizabeth
the angel's news.

She went to Elizabeth's house
for a visit.

"Elizabeth!" called Mary. "I am here!"

Elizabeth's baby jumped inside her, and
God's Spirit filled Elizabeth with sudden joy.

"You will be the mother of my Lord!"
she told Mary.

How does Elizabeth know about my baby? wondered Mary. "My heart is happy," Mary said, "because God is my Savior."

Mary stayed with Elizabeth for a few months and then went home.

Soon Elizabeth's baby was born.

"We will name him John," said Elizabeth.

"What?" said her friends.
"You are not
naming him Zechariah,
like his father?"
They asked Zechariah,
"What would you like
to name this child?"

On a tablet,
Zechariah wrote,
"His name is John."

At that moment, Zechariah could talk again, and he began to praise God.

Everyone was amazed.
"What will this baby be when he is grown?"
asked people everywhere.

One Night in Bethlehem

from Luke 2

"The king wants to know how many people are in his kingdom," Joseph told Mary. "We must go to my hometown and be counted."

Mary patted her large middle. "Bethlehem is far away, Joseph," she sighed. "And the baby is due any day now."

"Please don't worry," Joseph told Mary. "God will watch over us."

The trip to Bethlehem
was long and dusty.
And Bethlehem was crowded.

Joseph tried to find a room
where they could stay.

"Sorry," said the innkeeper.
"Every room here is full."

But Mary and Joseph found
a warm, clean stable.
And there Mary's baby was born.

The baby
was a boy, Jesus,
just as God's angel
had said!

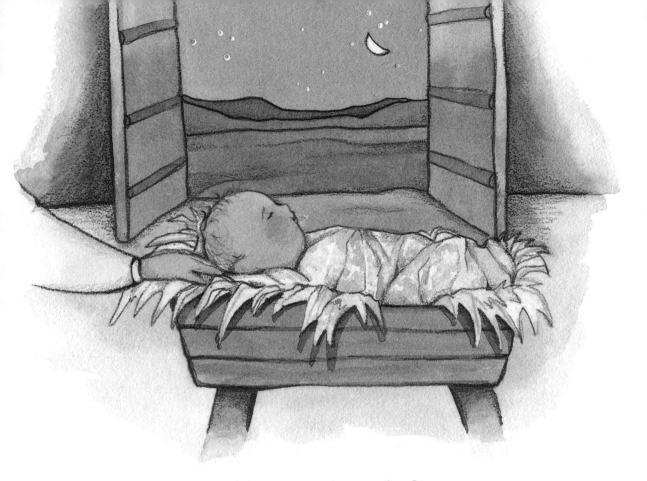

**Mary wrapped her newborn baby
in cloths to keep him warm.**

Tenderly she laid him in his first bed—
a simple feeding box
under the stars,
one night in Bethlehem.

Good News of Great Joy

from Luke 2

On the hills near Bethlehem,
shepherds watched their sheep.

Suddenly the night was bright!

And standing near the shepherds
was an angel of the Lord.

The shepherds were afraid!

But the angel said, "Calm down,
for I have come with good news of great joy!
Today in Bethlehem
a Savior has been born to you.
Christ the Lord has come!"

"You may go to see him,"
the angel told the shepherds.
"This will be a sign for you.
You will find the baby wrapped in cloths
and lying in a feeding box."

Then there were angels all around,
praising God and saying,
"Glory to God in the highest!
And peace to his people on earth!"

When the angels were gone,
the shepherds said,
"Let's go to Bethlehem!"

They hurried into town and found
Mary and Joseph and the baby,
just as the angel had said.

Then the shepherds
went back to their sheep,
praising God all the way.

Follow That Star!

from Matthew 2

Wise men from the east
came to Jerusalem.

"Where is the child
who was born
king of the Jews?"
they asked. "We saw his star in the east.
We have come to worship him."

King Herod was angry.
He wanted to be the only king!

He called
the Jewish leaders.

"Tell me where the Christ
will be born," he said.

"In Bethlehem," they told him,
"just as the prophet wrote."

"Go to Bethlehem," Herod told the wise men.
"Look for the child there.
When you find him, come and tell me.
I want to worship him, too."

But King Herod was lying.
He did not want to worship the baby.
He wanted to have him killed.

The wise men left for Bethlehem.
"Look!" they said. "There is the star again."

They followed the star
until it stopped right over
the house where Jesus was.

The wise men went inside.
They saw Jesus with Mary,
his mother.

172

They bowed down
to worship him
and gave him
precious gifts.

That night in a dream,
God sent a warning to the wise men.

"Do not go back
to King Herod,"
God said.

So the wise men
went home by
a different road.

Taller and Wiser

from Luke 2

When Jesus was 12,
he went with Mary and Joseph
to the Passover feast in Jerusalem.

Passover was a time to remember how God
had saved his people from slavery in Egypt.

When the feast was over,
Mary and Joseph and others
from their town began the trip home.

They thought Jesus was with them.

**At the end of the day, Mary asked,
"Where is Jesus?" No one knew.**

Mary and Joseph went back to Jerusalem.

They looked up and down
the streets of the city.

They found Jesus at the temple,
talking with the teachers.

Everyone
who listened
was surprised.

Jesus understood
so much about God
and his ways!

"Son," said Mary,
"why have you
made us search
for you?"

"Why were you
looking for me?"
asked Jesus.
"Didn't you know
I had to be
in my Father's house?"

**Then Jesus went home
with Mary and Joseph
and always obeyed them.**

**Mary often thought
about all these things.**

And Jesus kept on
growing taller and wiser,
pleasing all who knew him
and pleasing God.

The Right Thing to Do

from Matthew 3, Mark 1, and Luke 3

When John grew up,
he preached to God's people.

"Get ready!" he told them.
"Change how you live.
The kingdom of heaven
is coming soon."

At the Jordan River,
many people said,
"John, we are sorry
we have not obeyed God."

Then John baptized them
in the river.

Jesus came
to John
to be baptized.

But John knew
that Jesus
had never sinned.

"I need to be baptized by *you*,"
John said. "Why do you come to me?"

"It is important to baptize me,"
Jesus said. "It is the right thing to do."

So John baptized Jesus.

When Jesus came up from the water, heaven opened.

The Spirit of God came down like a dove and landed on Jesus.

Then a voice came from heaven.
"You are my Son,"
said the voice.
"I love you, and I am
very pleased with you."

Jesus' Team of 12

from Matthew 4, Mark 1 and 3, Luke 5 and 6, and John 1

Two brothers,
Peter and Andrew,
washed their fishing nets.

Jesus got into
Peter's boat.

"Go out to deep water," Jesus said.
"Put your nets into the water
so you can catch some fish."

"Teacher," said Peter,
"we fished all night.
We could not catch
any fish."

But Peter
obeyed Jesus
and put the nets
in the water.

Suddenly, the nets
began to break.
They were full of fish!

"Come and help us!"
called Peter and Andrew
to James and John
in another boat.

Soon both boats were so full of fish
that they began to sink.

Then Peter knew
that Jesus was from God.

"Don't be afraid," said Jesus.
"Follow me. From now on,
you will catch people, not fish."

Peter and Andrew left everything
and followed Jesus.
So did James and John.

And later Jesus also called Philip,
Bartholomew, Matthew, Thomas,
another James, Thaddaeus,
Simon the Zealot, and Judas
to be with him on his team of 12.

Inside and Out

from Matthew 9, Mark 2, and Luke 5

Jesus was teaching in a house.
A crowd of people filled the house to hear him.

Then four friends came,
carrying a man who could not move.

"This crowd is too big," the four men said.

So they took the man on his mat up on the roof.

The four men made
a hole in the roof.

They lowered
their friend down
into the house,
right in front of Jesus.

Jesus saw that the four men had great faith.

"Your sins are forgiven,"
Jesus told the man on the mat.

The teachers of the law
were thinking,
Who does Jesus
think he is?
Only God can
forgive sins!

187

Jesus knew what the teachers were thinking.

He asked them, "Is it easier to forgive sins
or to say rise and walk?"
Then Jesus told the man on the mat,
"Stand up. Take your mat and go home."

The man jumped up.
He picked up his mat
and walked out of the house, praising God.

Everyone was amazed. Jesus had healed
the man on the mat—inside and out!

Jesus the Teacher

from Matthew 5 – 7 and Luke 6

A huge crowd of people
gathered on a grassy hillside.

They had come to see Jesus.
Jesus sat down and began to teach them.

"Happy are the humble," Jesus said.
"Heaven belongs to them.
Whoever is sad will find comfort.
Whoever loves mercy
and peace pleases God."

Jesus looked into the faces of the crowd.

"Love your enemies," he said.
"Forgive those who do wrong to you."

Jesus also taught about money.

"Don't worry about getting rich
here on earth," Jesus said.
"Live to please God.
Someday he will reward
you in heaven.
Pray always," said Jesus.
"Seek and you will find."

Then Jesus told a story.

"Everyone who hears me today
and obeys me is like a wise man
who built his house on rock," he said.
"When the rain and wind came,
that house stood strong."

"But a foolish man built his house on soft sand," said Jesus.
"When the rain and wind came, his house fell down with a crash. Anyone who doesn't listen to me is like that foolish man."

Just Say the Word

from Matthew 8 and Luke 7

A Roman soldier had a
servant who was dying.

The soldier heard
about Jesus.
So he sent some
Jewish leaders
to ask Jesus for help.

The leaders found
Jesus. "Please come
and heal the servant
of this soldier. He has
been good to us."

"I will come," said Jesus.

Soon Jesus and the Jewish leaders were close to the soldier's house.

The soldier sent out some friends with a message for Jesus.

This was the soldier's message:
"I am not good enough to have you
in my house. Just say my servant
is healed and he will be healed."

Jesus turned to the people following him.

"This Roman soldier has very great faith,"
he said. Then Jesus said to the soldier's friends,
"Go back to the house.
What you have asked will be done."

The soldier's friends
went back to the house.

They opened the door
and saw the soldier.

And next to him
was his servant,
who was
completely well!

Wild Winds and Waves Obey

from Matthew 8, Mark 4, and Luke 8

Jesus was tired.
All day long
he had been
teaching from
a boat on the lake.

When evening came,
Jesus said to his disciples,
"Let's go over
to the other side of the lake."

In the back of the boat,
Jesus went to sleep.

Then a wild storm began.
The wind howled, and waves
came over the sides of the boat.

"We are in danger!" cried the disciples.

The disciples woke up Jesus.

"Teacher, Teacher, save us!"
they cried. "Don't you care
that we are going to drown?"

Jesus got up.
He turned to the roaring waters.
"Quiet!" he said. "Be still!"

The wind went away.
The waves were still.

Jesus said to his disciples,
"Why are you so afraid?
Where is your faith?"

"What kind of man is this?"
the disciples asked each other.
"Even the wind and the waves obey him!"

Enough for Everyone

from Matthew 14, Mark 6, Luke 9, and John 6

Jesus and his disciples were busy.

"Take away my sickness,"
said a man.

"Heal my son," said a woman.

Jesus and his helpers did not rest.

"Get into this boat," said Jesus. "We will go
to a quiet place on the other side of the lake."

The people ran around the lake
to meet Jesus there.

But Jesus was not angry.
"Bring the sick to me," he said.

Late in the afternoon,
Jesus' disciples said,
"Send the people to town for food."

"No," said Jesus. "We will feed them."

Andrew found a boy
with five loaves of bread
and two small fish.

"But that is not enough to feed a crowd,"
said Andrew.

"Tell the people to sit on the grass,"
said Jesus.

Jesus thanked God for the food.
He broke the bread and fish into pieces.

"Give the food to all the people,"
Jesus told the disciples.

Five thousand men, plus women
and children, had enough to eat.

The leftovers filled 12 baskets.

"Jesus must come from God," the people said.

Then Jesus quietly went
up the mountainside to pray.

Peter Takes a Walk

from Matthew 14, Mark 6, and John 6

"Take the boat to the other side of the lake," Jesus told his disciples. "I will meet you later."

Jesus went up into the hills to pray.

The disciples obeyed Jesus. But a mighty wind began to blow.

It blew against the boat as the disciples tried to row.

Jesus prayed a long time. Then he went down to the shore and began to walk across the water toward the boat.

The disciples thought they were seeing a ghost. "It is I," called Jesus. "Don't be afraid!"

But Peter called out, "Lord, if it is really you, tell me to come and meet you."

"Come!" said Jesus.

Peter stepped out of the boat and began to walk to Jesus on the water.

But the wind and waves pushed and pulled at him.

Peter was afraid, and he began to sink. "Lord, save me!" he cried.

Jesus reached out to Peter and helped him back into the boat.

"Why did you begin to doubt?" said Jesus.

Jesus got into the boat, too.
And the wind stopped!

Jesus' disciples worshiped him in the boat.

Now I See

from John 9

Jesus saw a man
who had been born blind.

The disciples asked Jesus,
"Is this man blind
because he sinned
or because his
parents sinned?"

"No," said Jesus.
"It is so that God's power
can be shown in him."

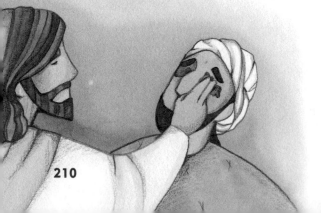

Jesus spit on the ground
and made some mud.
He put the mud
on the blind man's eyes.

"Now go wash
in the pool of Siloam,"
Jesus told the man.

The blind man did
what Jesus told him.
And he could see!

"Isn't this the man
who was blind
from birth?"
said the neighbors.

"How did this happen?" asked the teachers.

"Truly the one
who healed me
is from God,"
said the happy man.

But the teachers
did not want to believe it.

Jesus found
the man again.

"Do you believe
in the Son of Man?"
asked Jesus.

"Who is he?" said the man.

Jesus smiled. "You have seen him now,
and he is the one talking to you."

"Lord, I do believe in you!"
cried the happy man.

"I came into this world
so that many
will believe,"
said Jesus.

213

A Neighbor Shows Kindness

from Luke 10

A teacher of the Jewish law
came to Jesus
with a question.

"God's law tells me to love God
with all my heart, my soul, my strength,
and my mind. And to love my neighbor as myself.
But who is my neighbor?"

So Jesus told this story.

A man was traveling down
a rough and rocky road.

Then robbers grabbed him,
took his clothes,
and beat him.

They left him lying on the road.

A priest came along the road.
He saw the hurt man.

But he went by on the other side.

A temple worker came along the road.

He saw the hurt man, too.
But he went by on the other side.

A man from Samaria came along the road.

Jews did not like Samaritans.
But this Samaritan stopped.

He cleaned the hurt man's wounds
and put on bandages.
Then he took the man to an inn.

The Samaritan had to leave
the next day.

But he used his own money to pay the innkeeper.

"Look after this man," he said to the innkeeper. "If you need more money, I will give it to you when I come back."

Then Jesus asked the teacher of the law, "Which of the three travelers was a neighbor to the hurt man?"

"The one who helped him," said the teacher of the law.

Jesus said, "Go and do the same."

Teach Us to Pray

from Matthew 6 and Luke 11

Jesus was praying.

When he was done,
one of his disciples said,
"Lord, please teach us to pray."

Jesus gave his disciples
a prayer for an example.

"When you pray," said Jesus,
"pray like this."

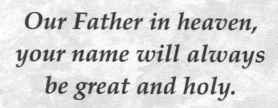

Our Father in heaven,
your name will always
be great and holy.

Be our king!
Set up your heavenly kingdom
here on earth.

Give us our food for today.

Forgive our sins.
And help us forgive others
who have done wrong to us.

Jesus finished the example prayer with these words.

Lead us away from wanting to do wrong things.

Free us from the evil one.

Because the kingdom is yours, with power and glory forever. Amen.

Lost and Found

from Luke 15

Jesus told this story. A man's younger son asked for his share of the family money.

Then he left home. The young man wasted all his money.

When his money was gone, no one would give him anything.

The only job he could find was feeding pigs.

He was so hungry that even the pigs' food looked good to him.

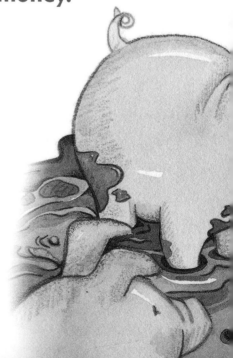

"My father's servants
have food to eat,"
said the son. "I will go back
to my father
and be one of his servants."

While the young man
was still a long way
from home,
his father saw him.

The father ran to his son and hugged him.

"Quick! Give him the best robe," the father told his servants. "Put a ring on his finger and sandals on his feet. Prepare for a party! My son has come home!"

Then the young man's brother came in from the fields.

"Come to
the party,"
the father said.

**"No," said the brother.
"You have never given
a party for *me*."**

"But you are
always with me,"
said the father,
"and everything
I have is yours.
We had to have
a party, because
your brother,
who was lost,
has been found!"

Lazarus Lives Again

from John 11

Lazarus, who lived in Bethany, was very sick.

Mary and Martha, his sisters, sent someone to tell Jesus, "Your friend Lazarus is sick."

But Jesus stayed where he was for two more days.

When Jesus came to Bethany, Lazarus was dead.

"Lord," said Martha, "if you had been here, my brother would not have died."

"Your brother will live again," said Jesus. "I am the resurrection and the life. He who believes in me will live."

"I believe you are the Son of God," said Martha.

Then Mary came to Jesus
and fell at his feet
and said, "Lord, if you had been here,
my brother would not have died."

Mary and the friends with her were crying.

Jesus was very sad.

"Where have you laid
Lazarus?" he asked.

They showed him
the place.

Jesus cried. Then Jesus said, "Take away the stone." He called out in a loud voice, "Lazarus, come out!"

And Lazarus came out, alive.

"Take off the grave clothes," Jesus said, "and let him go."

One Thankful Man

from Luke 17

Jesus came near a village between Samaria and Galilee.

There he heard a loud cry, "Master, please help us!"

Jesus saw ten men standing by themselves.

They had a terrible skin disease called leprosy.

No one wanted them around.

But Jesus was not afraid of the sick men.
He wanted to help them.

"Go show yourselves to the village priests,"
Jesus told them.

The ten men obeyed Jesus.

And as they were walking to find the priests,
suddenly their sores disappeared!

One of the men ran back to Jesus.
He bowed down at Jesus' feet.

"Oh, thank you, Master!" he cried.

And he was a Samaritan, not a Jew
like Jesus and the disciples.

Jesus looked around. "Where are the others?"
he asked. "Did I not heal *ten* men?
Is this Samaritan the only one
who gives praise to God?"

Then Jesus smiled at the man and said,
"Get up and go now.
You were healed because you believed."

Let the Children Come

from Matthew 19, Mark 10, and Luke 18

Some mothers and fathers came to Jesus.

They carried babies in their arms.

They held their boys and girls by the hand.

"We want Jesus to pray for our children," the mothers and fathers said. "We want Jesus to give them his blessing."

But Jesus' disciples tried to stop the mothers
and the fathers.

"Get back!" they said.
"Can't you see that Jesus is busy?
He does not have
time for children!"

Jesus heard his disciples.
He reached out his arms
and called to the children.

"Let the children come to me," he said.
"Don't stop them."

Jesus told his disciples,
"The kingdom of God
belongs to children like these!
Everyone needs
the simple faith of a child
to enter the kingdom."

Jesus hugged the boys and girls.

He held the babies.

And to the delight of the mothers
and fathers, Jesus laid his hands
on all the children and blessed them.

237

Big News for a Little Man

from Luke 19

Zaccheus the tax collector felt squished.

He wanted to see Jesus.
But no one liked a tax collector.

No one would let Zaccheus
through to the front of the line.

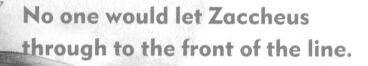

Then Zaccheus had an idea.

He climbed a tree!

"Hello, Zaccheus,"
said a gentle voice.

Zaccheus looked
down. The voice
belonged to Jesus!

"Come down quickly," said Jesus.
"I must stay at your house today."

"At *my* house?"
said Zaccheus.

"Of course," said Jesus.

Zaccheus was happy.
He welcomed Jesus
to his house.

People in the crowd were saying,
"Zaccheus is a bad man!
Jesus has gone
to the house
of a liar
and a thief!"

"What the people say is true,"
Zaccheus told Jesus. "I have cheated people.
But I am sorry."

"I know," said Jesus. "That is why I came."

Zaccheus decided to make things right.

"I will share with the poor," he said.
"And I will pay back everyone I cheated.
I will give back extra money besides."

Jesus was pleased.
"This is a good-news day," he said.

Praise to the King of Kings!

from Matthew 21, Mark 11, Luke 19, and John 12

Jesus and his disciples
came to a village near Jerusalem.

"Go into the village," Jesus said to
two disciples. "You will see a donkey
and her colt. Bring the colt to me."

The disciples did what Jesus said.
Some people asked, "Why are you taking that colt?"

"The Lord needs it,"
the disciples said.
"He will send it back later."

The disciples brought
the colt to Jesus.

They spread their coats
on the colt's back.
Jesus sat on the colt.

A large crowd gathered.
Some spread their coats
on the road
in front of Jesus.

Others spread palm branches
from the fields
along the road.

Jesus rode toward Jerusalem.

Some of the people in the crowd
went ahead of Jesus.

Some of the people followed.

Everyone shouted, "Blessed is the one
who comes in the name of the Lord!
Blessed is the one who comes
from the family of David!"

Jesus entered Jerusalem like a gentle king.

Remember Me

from Matthew 26, Mark 14, Luke 22, John 13, and 1 Corinthians 11

On the night of Passover, Jesus and his disciples met in an upper room.

Jesus wrapped a towel around his waist.

Then he washed his disciples' feet.

"I served you by washing your feet," said Jesus. "You also must serve others."

During the meal, Jesus took bread. He said a prayer of thanks.

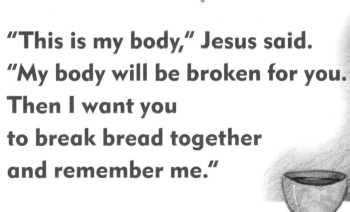

He broke the bread and gave it to his disciples.

"This is my body," Jesus said. "My body will be broken for you. Then I want you to break bread together and remember me."

Jesus took a cup. He said a prayer of thanks
and gave the cup to his disciples.

"This cup is a new promise," he said.
"When I die, my blood will be poured out for you.
Then I want you to drink the cup together
and remember me."

Jesus and the disciples sang a hymn together before they left the upper room.

A Sad, Dark Night

from Matthew 26, Mark 14, Luke 22, and John 18

Jesus and his disciples went to a garden.

"Sit here while I pray," he said.

Jesus walked ahead.
He took Peter, James, and John.

"My soul is full of sadness," Jesus said.
"Stay here and keep watch."

He walked
a little farther.

"Father, you can do anything," he prayed. "Take this suffering away. But do what you want, not what I want."

An angel came to Jesus to help him.

Three times Jesus prayed. Each time when he went back to Peter, James, and John, they were asleep.

"Peter," he said, "stay awake and pray."

When Jesus came back the third time, he said, "Are you still sleeping? The hour has come."

Soldiers came into the garden.
They grabbed Jesus.

"I know this must happen," Jesus said.
"What the prophets wrote about
must come true."

So the soldiers took Jesus away.
And Jesus' disciples were afraid.

King of a Different Kingdom

from Matthew 27, Mark 15, Luke 23, and John 19

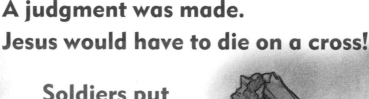

A judgment was made.
Jesus would have to die on a cross!

Soldiers put
a purple robe
on him. They put
a crown of thorns
on his head.

Making fun of him, they
said, "Here is the king."

Then Jesus had to carry
a heavy wooden cross
to a hill called Calvary.

A crowd followed him.

On the cross, Jesus said, "Father, forgive them. They do not know what they are doing."

Two robbers hung on crosses beside Jesus.
"Jesus, remember me when you are king," said one.

"Today you will be with me in my heavenly kingdom," Jesus told him.

Then darkness covered the whole earth.

Jesus called out in a loud voice, "Father, I give myself to you!" And Jesus died.

At that moment, the temple curtain
in Jerusalem ripped in half.

The earth shook and rocks split.
The soldiers at the cross said,
"Surely he was the Son of God!"

A rich man named Joseph
wrapped Jesus' body in clean linen cloths.

He put the body into a new tomb.

Then a big, heavy stone was rolled
in front of the tomb to close it tight.

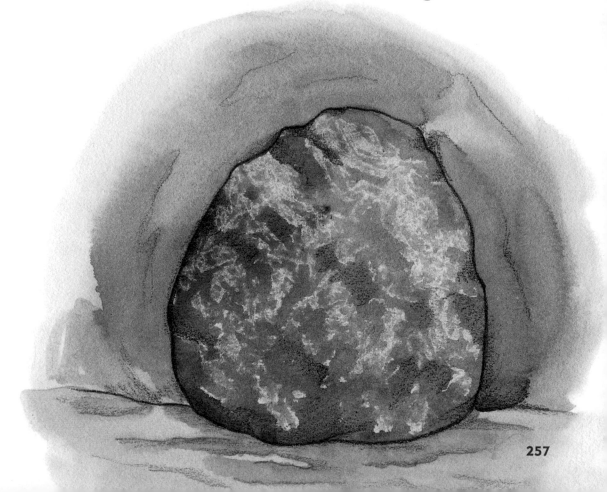

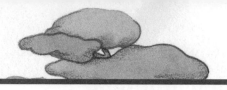

Could It Be True?

from Matthew 28, Mark 16, Luke 24, and John 20

It was the first day
of the week.
The sun was coming up.

Mary Magdalene
and the other women
went to Jesus' tomb.

They carried sweet-smelling spices
to place around Jesus' body.

"How will we get into the tomb?"
asked one of the women.
"Who will roll the stone away?"

But when the women got there,
the stone was rolled away already!
An angel from God had done it.

The women walked into the tomb.
Jesus' body was gone!

Mary ran to tell
Peter and John.

Then two angels came
to the other women.

"Don't be afraid,"
the angels said.
"You are looking
for Jesus.
But he is not here.
He has risen!"

The women
hurried away
to tell the disciples.

After the women were
gone, Peter and John
came running.

The tomb was empty,
just as Mary had said!

Then John believed
that Jesus was
alive again.
But Peter wondered.

It Is True!

from Luke 24 and John 20

Mary Magdalene went back to the empty tomb.

She was crying.
What had happened to Jesus?

"Why are you crying?"
she heard someone ask.

Mary thought it was the gardener.

Then Mary heard her name.
The one talking to her was Jesus!

"Teacher!" cried Mary.

Mary ran to tell the disciples
that she had seen the Lord.

The other women were on their way
to tell the disciples what the angels had said.

Suddenly, they met Jesus!

"Don't be afraid," he told them.
"Go and tell my disciples to go to Galilee,"
Jesus said. "They will see me there."

The women
hurried
to find
the disciples.

That evening, all the disciples
except Thomas were together
in a locked room.
Suddenly Jesus was with them.

"Peace be with you!" Jesus said.
The disciples were filled with joy.

And a week later, Thomas saw Jesus, too.
"My Lord and my God!" said Thomas.

Parting Promises

from Matthew 28, Luke 24, and Acts 1

Jesus stayed on earth for 40 days after he arose.

On a hill in Galilee, Jesus told the disciples,
"You will receive power.
Go to all the nations.
Make disciples everywhere.
Baptize them in the name
of the Father, Son,
and Holy Spirit."

"Teach them to obey everything I have taught you. I will be with you always."

On his last day on earth, Jesus led the disciples to the Mount of Olives.

He lifted his hands to bless the disciples.

While he was blessing them, Jesus went up into heaven.

The disciples kept looking up until he was hidden by a cloud.

**Then two men dressed in white
stood beside the disciples.**

"Why are you looking into the sky?"
they asked. "Jesus has been taken
from you. But he will come back
just as you have seen him go."

Then the disciples went back to Jerusalem with great joy.

And they stayed in the temple, praising God.

The Very First Church

from Acts 2

On the Jewish holiday called Pentecost,
the disciples met together
in a house in Jerusalem.

A sound like a strong wind
suddenly filled the house.

Then what looked like tongues of fire
rested on the disciples.

270

God's Holy Spirit filled the disciples.

They began to speak in other languages.

People heard the noise
and gathered around the house.

"What's going on?" they asked.

Everyone could hear his own language being
spoken, even the people from other lands!

Peter said, "Listen! What the prophet Joel
wrote about is happening today:

> 'God says, I will pour out my Spirit
> upon all people. And everyone
> who trusts in the Lord will be saved.'"

"Jesus was killed," said Peter.
"But God made him alive again.
We have seen him! He is in heaven now.
Jesus is the Christ, the one God promised to send."

> The crowd gasped.
> "What shall we do?" they asked.

"Repent," said Peter.
"Be baptized for the forgiveness of your sins.
And you will receive the gift of the Holy Spirit."

Three thousand people believed in Jesus and were baptized that day!

Jumping for Joy

from Acts 3

Peter and John went to the temple to pray.

At the temple gate sat a man
who could not walk.

Every day, his friends carried him
to the gate to sit and beg.

The man asked
Peter and John
for money.

"I have no money," said Peter. "But I have something else. In the name of Jesus, rise and walk!"

Peter grabbed the man's hand and began to help him up.

Right then the man was healed. He jumped to his feet and began to walk.

He went into the temple courtyard
with Peter and John, walking and jumping
and praising God.

People came running
to see the man.
"This is the one
who used to beg,"
they said.
"What has happened
to him?"

"Don't stare at *us*," said Peter.
"We did not heal this man."

"This man was healed by the power of Jesus,"
said Peter. "Jesus was killed on the cross.
But God made him alive again,
and we have seen him!
He is with God in heaven now,
just as the prophets said."

Saul Sees the Light

from Acts 9

Saul did not want anyone
to believe in Jesus.

He went to the high priest.

"Let me arrest any believers
I find in Damascus," Saul said.

Then Saul set out for Damascus.
But on the way there,
suddenly a light
from heaven flashed.

Saul fell to the ground.
He heard a voice say,
"Saul, Saul,
why are you hurting me so?"

"Who are you, Lord?" asked Saul.

"I am Jesus,"
said the voice.
"Get up now and go
into the city. Someone
will tell you what to do."

When Saul got up, he was blind.
His friends led him into the city.

God sent a man named Ananias to the house
where Saul was. Ananias laid his hands on Saul.

"The Lord Jesus
sent me so you
can see again
and be filled
with the Holy Spirit."

Then Saul could see again.
He got up and was baptized
as a new believer in Jesus.

Saul began to preach to the Jews in Damascus.
"Jesus is truly God's Son," he told them.

"Isn't this the man who arrests believers?"
the Jews asked each other.
"What has happened to him?"

Timothy Joins the Journey

from Acts 15 and 16 and 2 Timothy 1

Saul became known as Paul.

Paul traveled from place to place, preaching about Jesus.

In each town, the new believers met together as a church.

Paul wanted to see if the new churches were growing.

So Paul and his friend Silas traveled to Galatia.

There they stopped at a city called Lystra.

They visited a young believer named Timothy.

Timothy's mother and his grandmother were believers, too.

Paul had a question for Timothy.

"We are traveling to visit the new churches," Paul told him. "Will you come with us?"

Timothy was happy to join the journey.

So Paul, Silas, and Timothy
traveled together
to cheer the churches
and tell others about Jesus.

Paul learned to love young Timothy
like a son.

And the churches
grew stronger in faith,
with new believers added every day.

The Night the Prison Shook

from Acts 16

Paul and Silas went to Philippi.

They preached about Jesus.

But they were arrested by angry people who didn't want to hear about Jesus.

"Beat them," said the judges. "Put them in prison. And don't let them escape!"

286

The prison guard put chains
on Paul and Silas.
He put their feet in stocks.

But at midnight Paul and Silas
were singing and praying out loud.

The other prisoners heard them.
Suddenly, an earthquake shook the prison.

All the doors flew open.
Everyone's chains broke loose.

The guard woke up. He was afraid.
Had his prisoners escaped?

"Don't worry!"
shouted Paul.
"We are all here."

"What must I do to be saved?"
asked the thankful guard.

"Believe in the Lord Jesus,"
said Paul and Silas.
"He will save you and your whole family."

Paul told the guard and his family more about Jesus.

The guard washed Paul and Silas's wounds.

Then he and his family were baptized. He was filled with joy!

Come Quickly, Lord Jesus!

from Revelation

John was arrested for teaching about Jesus.

He was sent to live on an island called Patmos.

God gave John visions while he was on the island.

In one vision, John saw Jesus.

"Write on a scroll what you see,"
Jesus told him. "Send it to the churches."

John also saw heaven. There he saw
angels around God's throne
and every creature in heaven and earth
singing praise to God and Jesus.

Out of heaven came a new city,
made of gold and precious gems.

A crystal-clear river flowed
through the city, and God's throne was there.

"There is no sun or moon," wrote John. "The glory of God gives it light."

In the new city, John heard a loud voice from God's throne.

"Now God will live here with his people. He will wipe every tear from their eyes. There will be no more death or crying or pain."

"I am coming soon," Jesus told John.

Come quickly, Lord Jesus!

Look for these other
Read Together books!

0-7847-1742-7

0-7847-1743-5

0-7847-1738-9

Visit your local Christian bookstore
or www.standardpub.com or call 1-800-543-1353.